SEXES

SEXES

THE MARRIAGE DIALOGUES

SAMUEL HAZO

TRIQUARTERLY BOOKS
NORTHWESTERN UNIVERSITY PRESS
EVANSTON, ILLINOIS

TriQuarterly Books
Northwestern University Press
www.nupress.northwestern.edu

Some of the poems in this book appeared first in *The Holy Surprise of Right Now* (University of Arkansas Press, 1996) and *Just Once* and *A Flight to Elsewhere* (Autumn House Press, 2002 and 2005).

Printed in the United States of America

10 9 8 7 6 5 4 3 2 1

Library of Congress Cataloging-in-Publication Data
Hazo, Samuel, 1928– author.
    Sexes : the marriage dialogues / Samuel Hazo.
        pages cm.
    ISBN 978-0-8101-5245-8 (pbk. : alk. paper)
    I. Title.
    PS3515.A9877S49 2014
    811.54—dc23

2013046187

∞ The paper used in this publication meets the minimum requirements of the American National Standard for Information Sciences—Permanence of Paper for Printed Library Materials, ANSI Z39.48–1992.

Contents

Preface

It may seem redundant to state that men act differently in the company of women than in the company of men. But they do, just as women act differently in the company of men than in the company of women. The dialogues in this book are concerned with the dramas, both casual and profound, that occur when husbands and wives confront one another at life's various intersections. It is at these moments that the differences in gender, which is what sex is understood to mean in most dictionaries, on check-box forms, and in daily life, reveal themselves.

S.H.

SEXES

The Banterers

"Now here's a politician says he
    knows the mind of South
    America," he muttered as he read,
    "How's that for modesty?"
                              She had
    the look of someone studying
    her favorite piece of jewelry
    alone.
                    He crunched the pages
    of the paper like excelsior.
                                  "Ads,
    ads, ads—you need a microscope
    to find the news."
                          She smiled
    and asked, "Do you remember what
    happened thirty years
    ago today?"
                    "The Yankees won
    the pennant?"
                      "No."
                                    "Armstrong
    claimed the moon for Nixon?"
"No."
        "I bought that clinker
    of an Oldsmobile?"
                          "You asked me
    to marry you."
                    "And what was your answer?"
"I refused."
            "Why?"
                        "Cary Grant
    asked me first."

"What made you
change your mind about him?"
"You."
        "Me?"
                Just then
she noticed it—a small white
box no larger than a domino
beside the telephone.
                        "What's
in the box?"
                "Maybe it's something
from Cary Grant."
                        After opening
the velveteen lid, she plucked
the ring and eased her finger
into it.
                She posed.
                        He focused
on the team standings in the National
League West.
                        She let the ring
bewitch her as she modeled it
and hummed.
                "Cary?"
                                "Yes."
"You'll have to help me take
this off."
                "I'll try," he said
and reached for the ring.
                        "Not that,"
she said, guiding his hand
to the belt of her robe, ". . . this."

A New Deal

"Who says we need a new car
    now, right now, today?"
For her a car was transportation,
    nothing more.
                    "This wreck
    burns oil, and the warranty's
    expired."
                    "Why not renew it?"
"I want a new car pronto,
    this minute—end of discussion."
It was election day plus one.
The whole country had swung
    to the right.
                    He felt betrayed.
"I'll never understand," she said,
    crossing her fingers, "why men
    and cars are just like *that*."
He drove on automatic pilot,
    tallying the radio returns
    from Maine to Texas through the whole
    catastrophe.
                    "Your mind is always
    elsewhere when you drive,
    and that's not safe."
                    "The country's
    gone to hell, and all you talk
    about is me, me, me."
"I'm not married to the country."
He turned the radio knob
    a click.
                    More tallies, more defeats . . .
He switched to the golden oldies.

"If you're set on getting a car,
    I hope the color is puce."
"Nobody makes a puce car."
"What about lavender with cream
    appointments?"
                        He looked at her
    as if she'd lost her mind.
Glenn Miller's "In the Mood"
    embalmed him in a sulk.

                        For just
    that long he thought of times
    when cars were only black,
    blue, or gray, and lavender
    described a sunset or a dress,
    and politics made his kind of sense.
"All right," she said, "I'll take
    apache red with pink leather."
That made him mad enough
    to spit.

                The He inched the window
down, turned halfway to his left
and spat all over his chin.
Hearing her laugh, he tried
    to stay quite serious.

                        "Not
funny," he said but found himself
laughing along with her,
and neither could stop.

                        Later
they laughed themselves giddy
as drunks each time they brought
it up if politics was in the news
or not.

                They kept the car.

Settings

"Why are we doing all this?"
   he asked as he set the final
   plate on the Madeira tablecloth.
"All what?" she said with Waterford
   goblets in each hand.
                              "Fussing
   like this for a dinner when all
   we'll end with will be dirty dishes
   and full stomachs."
                              "Is that
so bad?"
                    "If the whole purpose
   is just to feed your face,
   why bother with the frills?"
"I can't believe you said that."
"You better believe it."
                              Planting
   each goblet in place, she scanned
   the table like a maître d' and smiled,
   "Feeding your face is not
   the same as dining."
                              "Tell me
the difference."
                         "Frenchmen say
   that dining actuates our five
   senses all at once, and nothing
   else does."
                    "Lovemaking comes close."
"I knew you'd mention that,
   but even lovers need the right
   setting, or all you have
   is 'Wham, Bam, Thank you, Ma'am.'"

"The problem with the French is why
    they think the wrapping and the bow
    are more important than the gift."

                                "Not *more*

but as much, and I'm for that."
"But what's the point?"

                        "The point
    is that the presentation makes
    a world of difference."

                            "Look

at your centerpiece—flowers
galore, and tomorrow they'll end
in the garbage can."

                            "But today
they're beautiful, and they enhance
the occasion."

                        "Here today,
gone tomorrow or sooner."

                            "Who

says longevity's the answer
to everything?"

                        "Who says it's not,
I'd like to know?"

                        "You miss

the point."

                        "*You* miss the point."

Two on the Fly

He's mad because the taxi's late.
She's certain she's forgotten something.
Enter the driver—all grins
  and Haitian and indifferent
  to the alphabet of indignation
  and their almost frantic, "Hurry, please!"
Once airborne, they relax
  until the turbulence.
                      He breathes
  in gulps, retches, and reaches
  for the paper bag.
                 She's absolutely
  sure there's something she's forgotten.
Landing, they learn their luggage
  never left America.
               They file
  a report, then shuttle into town . . .
Their room ". . . won't be available
  until . . ."
             They loiter in a lobby
  jammed with Japanese podiatrists
  on tour.
          She says she knew
  they never should have come.
He has the frown and stoop
  of someone stranded and friendless
  in Yokohama.
            Admitted to their room,
  she says she stressed twin beds
  and not a queen.

"You kick
all night, Jerome, and I
was looking forward to a rest."
"Beds are not just made
for sleep," he says.
                    "If that's
the only reason why
we're here, I'm going home
tomorrow."
          And she did.

Simon Says

He said, "The angles of our house
   remind me of solid geometry."
"Forget geometry," she scoffed,
   "I'll take the lawn and the roses."
Paging from news to the crosswords,
   he said, "A woman who fights
   bulls in Spain says strength
   is secondary to intelligence
   in bullfighting—the bull
   is always stronger."
                        "Any
woman who fights a bull
on foot," she said, "is dumber
than the dumbest bull."
                        "Who was
the conqueror who razed the cities
of his enemies and sowed the ground
with salt to keep them dead
forever?"
                "Who cares?" she huffed.
"You know," he said, "in heels
you walk like a pair of scissors
pointed down—closing
and opening."
                  "High heels flatter
a woman's legs," she said,
"and that's enough."
                    "The nude
bathers of Renoir look swell
without high heels."

"Too heavy
in the thighs," she smirked, "each pink
and tubby one of them."
                              "Adam
took Eve before heels
were invented."
                         "What choice did she have?"
"When you think about it," he said,
    "Eden was just a nudist camp."
"Don't think about it."
                         "Why?"
"I know where you're heading."
"Isn't loving meant to be fun?"
"Serious fun, but it comes
    in waves, and frankly I'm not
    feeling wavy at the moment."
Folding the paper, he said,
    "Tell me the opposite of maybe."
"Hell no or let's go,
    depending on my mood."
                              "I think
    it's time I called it a night."
"It's not even dark."
                         "From where
    I sit, it's getting darker
    by the minute."
                         "Tell me," she asked,
    "is wanting me the same as loving me?"
"What's the difference?
                         "One time
    you said your body's never yours
    until it's with my body."
                              "Did I
say that?"

"You said it *before*
and *after,* and it still makes sense."
"Sense or nonsense, it's the truth."
"I think I feel the same . . ."
"Before or after?"
"Now."

Every Weekend the Willises Go Away

Fingering her breasts for trouble,
 she hears him say, "I've yet
 to find out who I am."
        "You're
 Willis Willis, husband mine,
 and I'm your lawful bedded wife."
"Is Phyllis Willis who you really are?"
"The rhyme's a bummer, but at least
 we match."
      Without another word
 he dons his rainbow Reebok
 running shoes and jogs his daily
 dozen miles alone.
      Later
 when she gives herself to him
 reluctantly, she keeps on chewing
 popcorn and tells him to be quick.
Next day, leaving the Pekingese
 to sit the house, they pack
 the Jeep and head for the mountains.
"For me, home's always up ahead,"
 he says as he steers, "go,
 go, go—that's life."
       "Really?
 I thought that life's what happens
 when you stay at home."
       She thinks
 about her guest room with no
 guests, the stacks of china
 she has never used, the silver
 service tarnishing in cellophane.

She thinks about the Pekingese
    asleep on a cushion, surrounded
    by silence.
                The cabin greets them
    as they left it: an inch of last
    week's Pepsi in a paper cup,
    the toilet water filmed with ice
    like paraffin but flushable, the telephone
    he keeps refusing to connect.
"What happens, Will, if we need help—
    a helicopter, medivac?"
                        "The tough
    get going when the going
    gets tough.
                Dick Nixon did it—
so can we."
                That night
    they sleep like campers in their jeans.
She wakes at seven, sidles
    to the shower and slips on a tile.
Her ankle cracks like a twig
    in a bonfire.
                Two hundred
Jeep-miles later she's in pain
    and plaster of Paris.
                        "Just tough
    it out," he tells her when he leaves,
    "and we can still do Mexico
    in June or maybe Argentina—
    go, go, go."
                His words keep
    fading like a voice beyond the grave.
Nothing he tells her matters
    anymore.

She wonders who
this stranger is and how
they came to meet and why
she ever let him in her body.
The plastic bracelet on her wrist
reminds her of a handcuff.
She wants so much to sleep
like Snow White with a broken ankle
and awaken healed and changed
somewhere she's never been
as someone else—with someone else.

98.6

"I can't go through with this,"
   she said as she straightened the hem
   of her dress.
                  "Of course, you can,"
   he answered with a thumbs-up smile.
"Easy for you to say
   because you do this all
   the time . . . how's my hair?"
"Hair's fine."
                  "And my dress?"
                              "Perfect."
"You're just saying that."
                        Nothing
   he said had helped, and it
   had been that way for weeks.
"I never should have worn this dress."
"Forget the dress—it's you
   they voted for, and you
   they've come to hear."
                     "Where
   will you be?"
                  "Backstage, but I
   can still applaud."
                  "I can't
   remember my speech."
                     "If you
   forget, just improvise and say
   what's in your heart."
                  She turned
   to kiss him, then changed her mind.
"Is it good or bad luck to kiss
   before a speech?"

"Who cares?"
he said.
                    "If it's bad, we'd
better not."
            They eased
into the wings just as the chairman
introduced her.
                    "I'm suffocating
in this dress."
                    "Everyone's the same
Fahrenheit inside, so just
relax."
            She walked on stage
to loud applause, while he
stood back and listened as she spoke
without a note or flaw.
                        Exiting
to more applause, including his,
she stopped to receive a standing
ovation . . .
                Later he told her,
"I knew you could do it."
"Why not?" she said and let him
kiss her, "I told you I could
do it from the very beginning,
so why should you be surprised?"

Sex

"Forget the love scenes," he said.
"Which ones?" she answered, "Half
   the movie was one love scene
   after another."
                    "I counted five."
She shrugged as if the number
   made no difference, then asked,
   "How many people make love
   on the kitchen table, for God's sake?"
"How would I know?"
                    "Besides,
   there's too much showing
   plus all that huffing and puffing."
"I read somewhere that it's like
   nudism—everything displayed,
   nothing revealed."
                    "It's insulting
   to women, and I'm a woman."
She poured more coffee in his cup.
He said, "Not much is hidden
   anymore."
            "Not *anything.*"
                    "I guess
   you're right."
                    "My mother's mother
   never knew a thing until
   her wedding night, but still
   she had six children and was happy."
"I guess she learned as she went."
"What's more—when she was eighty-two
   she still believed adultery was just
   the opposite of infantry."

He laughed
and said, "That shows how men
and women differ where it comes
to sex."

She poured some coffee
for herself and said, "With men
it's all performance."

"What's wrong
with that?"

"Nothing, until they can't."
"Can't what?"

"Just when they get good
at it, they find it harder
and harder to do."

"Let's change
the subject."

"I guess it's just
a case of desire getting ahead
of ability."

"Let's change the subject."

Positions

"What's sex?" she asked, "without love?"
"What's love?" he said, "without sex?"
Such words were certain to perplex
 with him beneath and her above.

Rummagers

"Why are we keeping these?"
   he asked, hefting three pairs
   of high-heeled snow boots from a box.
"They'll come in handy when the snow
   gets deep."
              "But why three pairs?"
"They're different colors, Jack,
   to go with three different outfits."
"Look at how high they are
   and tell me when we ever had
   two feet of snow."
             "It's always
  possible."
         He flung the snow boots
near the box and sat and said,
   "We're here to rid the house
   of junk, or am I wrong?"
"Not wrong, just impatient,"
   she answered and stood akimbo.
"After six hours, we've thrown
   out nothing but a shredded shower
   curtain, a rubber bath mat,
   and a broken vacuum cleaner."
"That's a start."
         He got to his feet
  and huffed.
         She huffed him back
and said, "Is that your way
   of saying you're disgusted?"
                "Not just
  disgusted but tired and fed up."

"Why?"
          "Maybe it's time
we threw out dresses and coats
you haven't worn in thirty years."
"Why do you get so mad
    at me for saving things?"
"Accumulating is not the same
    as saving."
                "What do you want me
to do?"
            "When in doubt,
throw out," he said and pointed
to a rack of dresses sleeved
in plastic bags.
                    "I don't have
the heart to pitch what are still
good dresses!"
                "But never worn—
the price tags are still showing."
"Should I have worn them home
    from the store the way you do?"
"What's better—to wear what you buy
    or leave them to strangers when you're gone?"
"Well, I'm keeping every one of these
    if they're thirty years old or not."
"But you're not what you were
    when you bought them!"
                    "Yes, I am!"

The Higher Logic of Marital Discussion

"You always think that something
   will go wrong."
                     "And sometimes,"
   she said, "I'm right."
                              "I like
   to think that things will go
   as planned."
                  "And sometimes you're wrong."
With one hand on the steering wheel
   and one at ease he said,
   "But thinking in advance of all
   that could go wrong means never
   taking a risk."
                  She turned
   away to watch a fleet
   of seven mallards on an inlet
   by the road and asked him, "Why
   do ducks always move in formation?"
"Ducks," he shouted, "how
   did ducks get into this?"
"You never hear my side and never
   change your mind, so what's
   the point of arguing?"
                          "That's just
   because you know I'm right."
"Not right," she said, "just certain."
For several miles they watched
   the road before them disappear
   and change into the road behind them.
"You're just the same with people,
   trusting them before you really
   know them."

"I trust until
I have a reason to distrust," he answered.
"Well, I distrust until somebody
    earns my trust, and that's
    the way it should be."
"How can you live that way?"
She focused on the road with such
    attention that she frowned until
    the frown relaxed into a knowing
    smile, "Sometimes you pay
    the price for trusting."
                        "When?"
"Remember the time you lent
    two hundred dollars to Zach?"
"So what?"
                "You knew he'd never
    pay you back."
                "But now
    he stays away from me,
    and that's a bonus."
                        She lifted
    her hands and let them drop
    on her lap, "And what about that waitress
    at the Howard Johnson's half
    an hour ago?"
                    "What about her?"
"She was the worst waitress
    we ever had, and she was rude,
    but still you tipped her double
    what you normally tip."
                        "I wanted
    her to feel ashamed."
                    She lifted
    her hands and shook her head
    and huffed a louder than normal
    huff.

"Did you have to huff?"
She smoothed the wrinkles from her dress
and turned and stabbed him with a stare,
"I didn't have to—I *wanted* to."

Cassandra

"You never look ahead,"
   she said, "and that's your problem."
"I look around," he answered,
   "where else is there to look?"
"I mean anticipating things
   that could go wrong."
                  "You sound
   like someone selling insurance."
She brushed the toast crumbs
   from her bathrobe sleeve and sighed.
"Last week," he said, "I listened
   to a pro who sold a policy
   designed to cover drowning,
   collision, murder, everything
   from falling off a bridge to being
   killed by bees."
             "What's wrong
   with that?"
             "There's no defense
   against the worst, Louise."
"So you did nothing, right?"
"I almost bought two graves
   from him—two for the price
   of one."
          "Not funny, Herb."
"What's wrong with living fully
   in the present tense?"
             "It's not
   enough."
          "We eat and drink
   and work and sleep and brush
   our teeth in the present tense."

"There's more to life than that."
"We make love in the present
  tense, Louise."
              "That's different."
"Speak for yourself."
                Just then
  she saw a sluice of water
  sliding down the kitchen wall,
  then another, and another.
                    "God,"
  she screamed, "I left the water
  running in the tub!"
                He dashed
  upstairs, turned off the taps,
  and pulled the plug.
                She shed
  her robe and sopped the floor
  with it.
          He did the same
  with his pajamas.
              When everything
  was dry, they faced each other
  shamelessly as Eve and Adam
  in the present tense.
                "I'm sorry,"
  she said.
        "No reason to be,"
  he answered and kissed her.
"You stay so calm in a crisis,"
  she added as she hugged him close
  and kissed him back.
                "If you
  had thought ahead, this never
  would have happened," he said.

"If you had thought ahead
    and caulked the tub last week,
    the water never would have run
    downstairs."
                    He kissed her on the cheek.
"Who wins this argument?" she asked.
"Both of us."
                "Impossible."
                                "It's like
    two lovers making love, Louise—
    both win regardless—guaranteed."

Undertones

"Sometimes you tune me out."
He stopped reading and smiled
    at her, "Why would I do that?"
"I don't know why, but you do."
"I like to think I listen
    carefully, especially to you."
"You listen, but you don't hear me."
He tried to name what lurked
    behind her words: frustration,
    boredom, envy?

                      At times
    like this he thought not answering
    was best.

               "That's typical of you,
    she smirked, "to say nothing or leave
    the room."

                    "What's wrong with that?"
"It's what men do, but women
    know that one of Shakespeare's
    ladies said it best—'I'm
    a woman—what I think
    I say.'"

              "I say what *I* think."
"Two days later."

                  "Better
    late than . . ."

                He knew her mood
    would make her say she had
    to get away, that anywhere
    was better than here, that what
    she had was nil compared
    to what she lacked.

30

"Kenny
and Rose are always going
out or away somewhere,"
she said, "but you stay put
right here."
                    "Right here is where
we live, remember?"
                    "But you
do nothing to change the tempo,
and every woman likes surprises."
"Finding you was the best surprise
of my life, Marie, and I
love you for who you are,
not what you do or where
you want to go."
                    She turned
away to keep the tears
from showing, but the tears kept
coming when she said, "You always
do that."
            "Do what?"
                    He offered
her his handkerchief.
                    Accepting it,
she said, "You always say something
that makes me cry when all
I wanted was a good, old-fashioned fight."

How Married People Break and Make Up

He said, "I'm not ignoring you."
She called him a name.
                     He mumbled
what she thought she heard.
"And don't say a word about
   my mother, you egotist."
                     He held
   a single scrubbed potato
   in his hand and said, "I asked you
   for *another,* and your *mother*
   had nothing to do with it."
"Don't lie."
              He denied whatever
she denied whenever she denied
whatever he denied.
                  Meanwhile
   the dog hid in the pantry.
"You think more of the dog
   than you do of me."
                With that
she marched upstairs and shut
the bedroom door with a will.
When she returned to the kitchen,
   she was dressed for the street.
"I'm going to my sister's, so don't
   wait for me."
             "Dinner's
   on the table."
             "I hope you enjoy it."
"Remember Ernie Cavanaugh?"
She started to leave, then turned.

"What about Ernie Cavanaugh?"
"What about who?"
                "Ernie
   Cavanaugh—you brought it up!"
"I saw him at lunch with his wife,
   that's all, and they looked great."
"He couldn't look great because
   he's still in love with me."
"I doubt if anyone could stop
   being in love with you."
"Who is she?"
           "She said her name
 was Gretchen."
             "Gretchen?"
                    "Gretchen."
"Did Ernie ask about me?"
"So many times he made me think
   you married the wrong man."
"Don't ever say that."
             "Maybe
 it's true."
        "I'd never marry
 a man with dirty fingernails,
 and Ernie had dirty fingernails."
"I thought you were going to Ruth's."
"I changed my mind," she said
   as she sat across from him
   and added, "I can change my mind
   whenever I want to, can't I?"

How Married People Argue

Because they disagreed on nuclear
   disarmament, because he'd left
   the grass uncut, because she'd spilled
   a milkshake on his golf bag,
   he raced ten miles faster
   than the limit.
                    Stiffening,
   she scowled for him to stop it.
His answer was to rev it up
   to twenty.
              She asked him why
   a man of his intelligence would
   take out his ill temper on a car?
He shouted in the name of Jesus
   that he never ever lost
   his damn temper.
                She told him
   he was shouting—not to shout—
   that shouting was a sign of no
   intelligence.
             He asked a backseat
   witness totally invisible
   to anyone but him why women
   had to act like this.
              She muttered,
   "Men," as if the word were mouthwash
   she was spitting in a sink.
               Arriving
   at the party, they postponed the lethal
   language they were saving for the kill
   and played "Happily Married."

Since all the guests were gorging
　　on chilled shrimp, the fake went
　　unobserved.
　　　　　　She found a stranger's
　　jokes so humorous she almost
　　choked on her martini.
　　　　　　　　He demonstrated
　　for the hostess how she could
　　improve her backswing.
　　　　　　　　All the way
　　home they played "Married
　　and so what."
　　　　　　She frowned as if
　　the car had a disease.
　　　　　　　　He steered
　　like a trainee, heeding all
　　speed limits to the letter,
　　whistling "Some Enchanted Evening"
　　in the wrong key, and laughing
　　in a language only he could
　　understand.
　　　　　　At midnight, back
　　to back in bed, he touched
　　the tightness of her thigh.
　　　　　　　　She muttered,
　　"I'm asleep," as if her permanent address
　　were sleep.
　　　　　　He rose and roamed
　　the darkened house, slammed
　　every door he passed, and watched
　　a prison film with George Raft.
Abed at dawn, he heard
　　the tears she meant for him
　　to hear.
　　　　　　He listened and lay still.

Because they both had round-trip
    tickets to the past but only
    one-way tickets to the future,
    he apologized for both of them.
They waited for their lives to happen.
He said the hostess's perfume
    was Eau de Turpentine.
                            She said
    the party was a drag—no humor.
Word by word, they wove themselves
    in touch again.
                        Then silence
    drew them close as a conspiracy
    until whatever never was
    the issue turned into the nude
    duet that settled everything
    until the next time.

Body Language

"How's your headache?" she asked.
"Easing," he answered, "but I'm
     fighting it."
                    "How do you fight
a headache?
                    For us women
pain is pain.
                    If we hurt,
we cry or scream or just
say so."
               "But that makes pain
the winner."
                    His eyes were strafing
the beach while she kept lotioning
her thighs.
                    They'd been in Cannes
for a week, and all their talk
was anatomical.
                    She blamed this
on the semi-nudes who flanked them
daily on the beach.
                    She said
the women were "mistakenly unclothed."
For him the girl on his right
     was one of hundreds to appraise.
"This goddess beside me," he whispered,
     "is feeling no pain whatsoever."
She glanced at the girl and muttered,
     "Meat with eyes."
                    "To you,
maybe, but she proves the female
body in its prime is beauty
at its best."

"We don't stay prime
for long, Josh."
"But while
it lasts, you're 'sport for Jove.'"
"All women work the same
inside, so don't be fooled
by the wrapper."
Quickly she capped
the lotion bottle with a twist
and snapped, "You men are boys
in men's clothing.
You love us
only from the waist down."
"I love you down and up
plus 'all the demesnes that there
adjacent lie.'"
"Thank you,
Mercutio."
"It's true."
"Then, why
do you leer at the mermaid beside you?"
"Because she's beautiful."
"Then what?"
"That's where it ends."
"I hate
to question your aesthetics, Josh,
but that's where it *starts*," she said
and stood, "so watch, and I'll show you
the 'ocular proof.'"
With that,
she turned, shucked off her swimsuit,
asked him to hold it and posed
like Cleopatra, Rosaline, and Desdemona
so that he and everyone would see
how bodily convincing she could be.

Essential Services

With two faucets feeding the same
   spigot, she blended and kept
   thinning hot with cold until
   she turned the water warm.
"From reservoir to pump to pipe
   to kitchen sink," she said.
"And then it's sewered back
   to river water to complete the cycle."
"Since you're an engineer, explain
   just where we'd be without plumbers?"
"Back to barreled rain and wells
   and chamber pots," he answered.
He kept perusing *The Economist*
   while she plucked out the plug
   and watched dishwater swivel
   down the drain.
                    "Plumbers
   have a lot of power, John."
"What power?"
                  "The kind that comes
   from overseeing the whole system."
"And they don't come cheap," he muttered.
"They need to unionize."
                    "Why unionize?"
"Because together they could strike
   worldwide and stop a war."
He tried to laugh her words
   away while something in him
   said a woman of conviction
   with a cause was undeterrable.
She said, "We all use toilets,
   don't we?"

"Who can deny that?"
"What happens when they're stuffed
    or broken?"
                    "Nothing happens."
"Exactly, so if plumbers strike
    to stop a war by leaving
    everything unflushable—no war."
He had no answer, and she knew it.
"Remember that play," she said,
    "when all those wives in Greece
    got sick of sending sons
    and husbands off to battle?"
"*Lysistrata.*"
                    "Remember what
    they did . . ."
                    "What Aristophanes
    assumed they did . . ."
                        "Assumed
    or not, they said no sex
    until the killing stops."
"So what's the point?"
                        "It proves
    essential services are unignorable."
"Blackmail by sex?"
                    "It stopped
    the war, didn't it?"
                    "Is that
    what sex and plumbing have
    in common?"
                    "It stopped the war."

Rank and Fool

"I hate to see soldiers
   marching in formation," she said.
"It takes discipline," he muttered.
"But what's the point?"
                   "The point
   is that it makes a group
   into a unit, teaches men
   to act on command, instills
   obedience."
             They'd had this talk
   too often to be ill prepared.
His time as a marine had left
   its mark—shoes buffed
   to a high polish, trousers
   creased to the cuffs, and haircuts
   militarily exact with judgments
   to match.
          Her tactic was to speak,
   then wait.
         "It's all a front,"
   she said, "so strangers can kill
   strangers—murder incognito."
"It's been that way since wars
   began."
        "Even courage
   doesn't matter," she continued,
   " . . . the side with the best weapons
   wins."
        "All wars are decided
   in the end by men with guns
   in their hands."

She stood and sashayed
to his chair and said, "I think
all wars should be fought naked."
He shook his head and laughed
in her face.
She repeated, "I think
all wars should be fought naked."
"What genius came up with that?"
"Just me—on my own."
"Forget it."
"No one would be able to fight
in the cold months, and in the hot
months no one could recognize
the enemy because everyone
would be in the same uniform."
"How can men make war naked,
for God's sake?"
"That's just
what I said."
"Say it again."
"You said it for me."
"I said
that men can't make war naked."
"And I agree."
He tried to laugh,
but the laugh never happened.
"Who gave you that idea?"
he asked and shrugged the shrug
of the self-entrapped.
"Your dad."
"My dad?"
"He told me once
that couples who argue naked
find ways to work things out."
"He said that?"

"It worked for us,
didn't it?"

"We're people, not armies!"
he shouted and turned away.
"I give you a logical, irrefutable
way to keep people from killing
one another, and you get mad."
"Why not?"

"You even agreed
with me a minute ago."
"I was just repeating what you said."
"What's wrong with what I said?"
"Men can't make war naked,
Rebecca!"

"Bravo!" she told him,
"I couldn't have said it better."

Sexes

"Whatever has to do with love,"
    she hummed, "is all that matters
    to me."
                He continued sanding
    the last walnut brace
    for a table he'd been assembling
    for months and said, "We agree."
"The fact that you agree makes you
    different from most men."
                            "How?"
"You make things with your hands,
    you read, you're not obsessed
    with money, class, competition,
    and the rest."
                Each time she spoke
    of men, she made him feel
    exempted.
                Why he never discovered.
"So many men," she resumed,
    "would love an airport or a building
    or a street named after them or else
    be resurrected as a statue or a stamp . . ."
He thought of iron generals
    on iron horses in the heart of Washington
    and smiled.
                "Women," she said,
    "don't give a hoot about that."
"I guess that lasting means less
    for women than living in the moment . . ."
"See what I mean?"
                        "About what?"

"About how different you are
from other men—the way
you look at things."
He tipped
both ends of the brace with glue
and locked it in position.
"What
do you think?" he asked.
"I think
you're one hundred percent right
about women."
"I mean the table—
how does it look?"
"It looks
like a good table."
"Furniture
is good when no one can see
what's holding it together."
"The same holds true for love
between two people, doesn't it."
"I suppose it does."
"Love
as glue . . . bonding . . . do you see
the connection?"
"If you say so,
I see it."
"I say so."

Post Partum

"It's something only a woman
   can do, and I wanted to prove
   I could manage on my own.
That's how I thought at the time.
Harry stayed close for what
   the midwife called support,
   but in the end it's only
   mother and baby, husband
   or no husband.
                Nobody
   chose my way but me,
   although my sister tried
   to talk me out of it.
She's at her best when she
   can make the worst of things
   by finding something to resent
   that lets her tell me that I'm wrong.
'Epidural is like Novocain.
When dentists drill your teeth,
   they numb you so you never
   feel the pain.
              Without a shot
   you'd be in agony.
              Why choose
the agony, and, if you do,
so what?
        Either way the tooth
gets filled, and that's the purpose,
right?
       What's true for teeth
is true for babies.

                    Forget
    the heroics.
                    Take the epidural.'
Maybe I should have listened,
    but I went with natural and practiced
    huffing and puffing and pushing
    and the rest.
                    My labor lasted
    thirteen hours.
                    Harry lasted
    for twelve until I told
    the nurse to make the poor man
    leave.
                    Watching him watching
    me was just too much.
                                Toward
    the end I felt the only way
    to kill the pain was if
    I died right there in the stirrups.
They wanted to call a doctor
    to help, but I said no.
Maybe he could have helped,
    but lying there wide open
    with only the nurses and midwife
    watching was one thing.
Having another man around—
    a total stranger, really—
    was just one man too many.
It would have made things worse
        to have him see me that way."

Duly Noted

"A man called yesterday
 and asked if I was a housewife."
"And?"
             "I listened and told him
 I'm not married to a house."
They were sitting on their porch,
 she on the glider, he
 in a chair.
             She was gliding
 higher than usual.
                    "For men
 we're either seen as adjuncts
 or bodies on call—nothing
 in between."
             "I see you
 as Barbara—what's wrong
 with that?"
             "But this Barbara
 doesn't have your options, John."
"Options?"
             "Opportunities, outlets . . ."
He leaned forward and smiled,
 "As a man I can do push-ups,
 make war, make out, make trouble—
 all kinds of good things."
She pushed the glider higher,
 "I'm saying that women live
 in a masculine world, John,
 and you're not listening to me."
She'd said these things before,
 and there was nothing he could do
 but nod.

"The influence of women
is never minor in this world,"
he said, "and you'd be wrong
to underestimate it."
                    "I don't,
but what we do is always
indirect—suggestions here,
entrapments there."
                    "But isn't
power always strongest
when it's indirect?"
                    "Maybe,
but it takes too much
imagination, too much time."
"What would you prefer?"
"Equality," she said and stopped
    the glider in mid-glide,
    "equality, equality, equality."
He leaned back in his chair
    and smiled a half-smile and said,
    "Barbara, if that's what you want,
    I have to tell you as a man
    equality's a long way down."

The Way It Usually Ends

"Why bother with reunions anyway?"
"Why—," she answered, "it puts you
   in your generation, that's why?"
"What's so good about that?"
She turned the television on,
   then turned it off and on
   and off again.
          "Why don't we
   just consider it a change
   of scene?" she asked.
            "You said
   the same thing last year."
"And we went, and we enjoyed it."
"We end up feeling like survivors,
   and we're fewer every year," he sighed
   and loosened his tie.
          "Maybe
   the fault's with you," she said.
"With me?"
       "You men just talk
   about your golf scores or how
   much hair you've lost, and that's
   just boring."
        "Hair's a sensitive
   issue with men."
         "But everyone
   knows that hair's a recessive
   male gene, so why not
   just accept it and let nature
   take its course?"

She flicked on
the television remote and watched
a promo for Viagra on the screen.
"And then there's that," she scoffed
and muted the message.
                              "You talk
as if you women are above
it all."
            "We think there's more
to life than golf scores, hair,
and sex."
            "So you let nature
take its course and leave it go
at that?"
            "I think we do."
"Is plastic surgery one way
of letting nature take its course?"
"Women have problems with gravity
that plastic surgery can help,
but you wouldn't understand that . . ."
"Where's the consistency?"
                              "Who says
we have to be consistent?"
"And what about cosmetics, perfume,
hair color, and the other tricks?"
She clicked off the remote, then smiled
her silencing smile and said
with total conviction, "And we use
and love every one of them."

Backlash

"Why did she call?"
                    "She said
     she wanted just to stay
     in touch," he answered and slipped
     the folded phone into his pocket.
"After five years?"
                    Before
     they chose each other, both
     had other options—she
     with a French pilot who chose
     at last to marry French,
     he with a coworker whose skills
     matched his so closely they became
     competitive.
                    "I noticed she called
     on your cell phone."
                    "She must
     have kept the number from when
     we worked together," he said.
"Is this the first call or . . ."
"The first and only, so let's
     forget it."
                    All during dinner
     neither said a word.
                    Clearing
     the dishes, she asked, "What
     is she doing now?"
                    "She has
     a name, Jan."
                    "All right,
     what is 'the name' doing
     these days?"

"I don't know."
"Honest?"
"Honest."
Returning
to the kitchen, she started stacking
the dishes as if she hated
dishes more than cancer.
"Save the pieces," he said.
Above the clatter of dishes,
she shouted, "I always thought
that marrying someone for life
meant marrying someone totally."
"Totality for sure, and, if
the gods are kind, longevity."
"You agree?"
"Absolutely."
"Then why
did you answer the phone
when Miss Yesterday called?"
"How did I know who was calling?"
She returned from the kitchen, drying
her already dry hands
with a paper towel.
He plucked
the towel from her and said,
"That dinner was your best yet."
"Stop using psychology on me."
"I love the totality and longevity
of everything you cook."
She took his hand and sat
sidesaddle on his lap and said,
"I wish I knew what makes
a woman act like this . . ."
"Let's forget about her."
"I'm talking
about *me*, not *her*."

"If you
don't know how women think
and act, how should I know?"
"What if Pierre called me,
what would you say?"

"I'd be
surprised."
"He liked me a lot."
"No doubt about that."
"He really
liked me a lot, Joe."
"Agreed."
She dropped his hand and stood,
"Is that all you have to say?"

Checkmates

She played to win.
     He played
 to play or pass the time.
Each time he saw a chance
 to win, he let it pass.
It made for peace.
      "In chess
 the strongest man's a queen,"
 she said and tapped her queen
 for emphasis.
     "Not just in chess,"
 he mumbled and castled.
       "Checkmate,"
 she claimed, moving her queen
 to close the trap.
     He looked
 at her and smiled, "I lose
 again."
    "Sometimes I think
 you lose on purpose."
      "Not true,"
 he lied.
    "Did she . . . did Janet
 play chess?"
     "Why bring her up
 again?"
    "She was the other
 woman for a while, remember?"
"There was no other woman."
"Did she play chess?"
      "She played."

"Did you let her win
    the way you let me win?"
"You're pretty sure I lost
    on purpose, aren't you?"
                    "Was she
good?"
            "As a matter of fact,"
he said and stood and stretched,
"she was very, very, very,
very good."
                He watched her slowly
box the chessmen, his
and hers, before she whispered
like a woman talking to herself,
"That was one *very* too many."

Poles Apart Together

"Women's weak points are jealousy
    and envy."
                "What's the difference?"
he asked and saucered his cup.
"Jealousy's not sharing what's yours
    with anyone, and envy's wanting
    what someone else is jealous of."
"And you think these are women's
    weak points?"
                "Most women
    would deny it, but it's true."
She put aside her crossword
    puzzle and closed her eyes.
Alone and at ease, they spoke
    the passionate grammar of mates
    with nothing to win or lose
    but truth itself.
                She opened
    her eyes and said, "I think
    most men expect too much
    from women."
                "How?"
                "You see us
    as muses or tarts, but that
    presumes we're either saints
    or bitches at heart."
                "Some poets
    claim you're both at once."
"Who?"
                "Byron believed
    a virtuous but wanton wife

would cure him of wenching, and Jarrell
inferred that many a man's
ideal is the 'Good Whore
who reminds him of his mother.' "
"That's just saying that every man
loves two women—one
that he imagines . . ."
                                  "And another
never to be born," he added
with a wink, and both of them
laughed.
                    "If that's the way
things are," she said, "we're permanently
poles apart—North
Pole you, South Pole me."
"But what if we press the round world
flat and make the two poles
meet in the middle?"
                            "Nothing
can press the world that way."
"Love can."
                "Did a poet write that?"
"John Donne."
                  "Well done, John Donne."

Fault Lines

"Why does sex draw people together
 when they're young," she mused,
 "but keeps them apart when they're
 older?"
                  "Be more specific."
"When we were thirty, we made
 love whenever we chose, but now
 we make love when we can."
"Blame it on age, I guess."
He loosened his cummerbund
 and snapped off his bow tie.
She shucked her heels and sagged
 on the sofa.
                  "The urge is there,"
 she sighed, "but nothing else is,
 and that's not fair."
                  "No argument
there," he nodded, dropped
 his tuxedo jacket on a chair
 and yawned.
                  "Is that your answer?"
"What prompted all this talk
 of lovemaking, especially now?"
"You."
        "Me?"
                  "Each time you danced
 with me tonight, you kept
 gawking at the younger women
 on the floor."
                  "Not gawking, just looking . . ."
"See, you admit it."

"If beautiful
women impress me as beautiful,
is that a fault or just
an occupational hazard?"
                              "You don't
look at me like that anymore."
He walked to her and kissed her
on the forehead.
                              "You're still my first
wife," he said, "for all these years."
"Years have nothing to do
with it," she answered and frowned,
"I want that old reckless passion
we used to have."
                              He kissed her
again.
              "I think that nurse
was right the day I had
my physical."
                              "The one who ordered
me to leave the room before
you said I was your husband?"
"She said 'you might as well stay—
you've seen it all anyway.' "
"Nothing like frankness."
                              She stood
and faced him, "That's the problem,
that's what kills everything!"
"What's that?"
                              "Familiarity, familiarity,
familiarity!"
                              "It hasn't bred
contempt, if that's what you mean."
"It's bred indifference, and that's worse."
She retrieved her shoes and wiped
her eyes with the back of her hand,

"I'm not a mystery to you
anymore."
                    "Leave mystery
to young lovers—they need it."
"But that's what I want to be!"
"Young or a lover?"
                    "Both."

She Who Has the Last Word

"I thought you were asleep."
She shifted on the gurney and smiled,
   "I've been prepped, but I
   wanted to stay awake
   to see you just in case . . ."
"In case of what?"
               "In case—
you never know."
                 "It's routine
surgery, Sue—no need
for valedictions."
             "Will you
and the boys be OK?"
               She gripped
his hand and squeezed it softly.
"You're the only mom we have,"
   he said, "but somehow we'll survive."
"I wouldn't be much of a mother
   if I didn't worry."
             Her hair
was netted loosely on the pillow,
   and a white sheet covered her.
"I had to give the nurses
   all my hairpins and my rings."
"Mothers aren't supposed to worry
   about things like that."
               "Why not?"
"They're trivia for women, that's all."
"You don't stop being a woman
   just because you're a mother."
"Which one takes priority?"

                                    "The one
who speaks last."
                                A surgical
nurse approached and said,
"We're ready for you, Susan."
Susan smiled slightly
    and looked at him so tenderly
    he felt wounded.
                            Tightening
her grip on his hand, she said,
"If anything happens, take care
of the boys."
                        "Nothing will happen."
"Promise."
                    "Nothing will happen."
"Promise."
                    "All right, I promise."
The nurse pushed the gurney
    slowly down the corridor
    toward a pair of automated
    doors.
                    The doors flared open
    like wings as Susan glanced back
    and whispered, "How do I look?"

RSVP

"Sophie," he called, "let's go."
She'd planned the whole event
    for months in secret: banquet
    reservations for classmates of his
    from sixty years ago,
    a special cake with eighty
    candles.
              "Sophie, it's late!"
To keep it a surprise the guests
    were sworn to silence.
                    Knowing
    he hated birthday parties,
    she described it as a private
    dinner with a few, close friends.
"Why do I need a dinner
    for everyone to know how old
    I am?"
           "Do it for me."
"You're three years younger."
"So what?"
           "You don't know
    how it feels."
              Such arguments
    went on for weeks, and twice
    he totally refused to go.
"Do it for me," she pleaded.
"Why should I do it for you?"
"Because I asked you, Abe."
                 "Don't
    ask me."

The secret burst
when the caterer called while Sophie
was shopping.
                    Abe answered the
phone, listened, and gasped, "Two
hundred responses for what?"
He waited and snapped, "I don't care
how many guarantees you need!"
Later she had to tell him
everything.
                    "You mean Morris
is coming from Alaska—and Irv
and Dave, I thought they were dead."
"Everyone who's not dead is coming."
"My God, from Alaska!"
                    From then
until the final minutes
he took charge.
                    "Sophie,
for Godssake, hurry up!"
She took deep breaths to calm
herself, cologned her wrists,
and hoped that there was nothing
she forgot.
                    "Sophie, we can't
be late for something like this!"
Finally, she marched downstairs,
her gown not quite adjusted
and her lipstick still unblotted.
"It's about time," he huffed.
"You," she muttered as she passed,
    "I'm not talking to you."

The Thrower and the Keeper

It's best when casual—a quick
   "I love you" while the coffee cools
   or when we pass each other
   in the hall.
                 Skywriting lovers
who proclaim "I love you"
   to the world mistake publicity
   for praise.
              Better the ways
of Cyrano who saved his praises
   for Roxanne alone.
                No Cyrano,
I do my best to thank you
   for your bravery of heart, your sense
   of who'd be hurt by what
   is said or left unsaid, your rage
   when something totally unjust
   is totally ignored.
              On basics
we agree.
          On trivia, not always.
I claim the Iroquois were right—
   "Travel light, travel far."
               You say
the things we chuck today
   we just might need tomorrow.
So there we are—the chucker
   and the saver—now against
   mañana.
          On trips you pack
for three eventualities—delay,
disaster, and death.

I pack
the clothes I plan to leave
behind, the socks I'll never
wear again, the books
I bring to give away . . .
                    To be exact,
you're two-thirds right.
                    When I
need dimes for tolls or parking
meters, presto! you produce
them from the pocket of your coat.
If I need dollars, presto! out
they pop like Kleenex from the selfsame
coat.
            And that trick works
with any coat.
                    You keep
a history of birthdays, wedding
dates, and anniversaries, and twice
that saved us from the worst
of all embarrassments.
                    You store
for years the sales receipts
I'd throw away, and once
that spared us a calamity.
                    I doubt
we'll change.
                    What leaves me edgy
makes you more assured, so why
adjust?
            I'll keep on lightening
our overload of blankets, towels,
issues of the National Geographic,
Christmas ribbons, drinking
glasses from a dozen different
sets, galoshes, photographs,

and stubs, discarding, I concede,
some quality in all that quantity.
You'll go on saving snapshots,
rubber bands, old programs
from Toronto and New York,
cancelled stamps from Italy
and Belgium, shillings, francs,
a ring too tarnished to be worn,
door keys for God-knows-which
hotels, outdated medicines
and, finally, I gratefully admit,
some quality in all that quantity,
including, in the process, me.

The Sum of One Plus One Is One

"Worry is a form of love,"
   she said and waited for an answer.
"No argument with that," he said,
   "and that holds true for grief
   as well—no grief, no love—
no worry, no love."
               "You mean
   we agree for once?"
             He nodded,
then shuffled the cards and dealt her
the ace of hearts.
         She turned
the ace so that the heart's tip
was aimed at him.
           "Are you
   telling me something?" he asked.
"I worry about you."
           "Why?"
"You work too hard."
            "I thought
   your words about worry were
   meant for the children, not me."
"Some of the words, not all . . ."
He replaced her ace of hearts
   in the pack, shuffled the cards
   accordion-style, and squared them
   in a tight, tamed deck on the table.
"You know," he began, "they say a mother
   worries first for the child who's away,
   or if all her children are home,
   she worries for the one who's sick,

or if they're well, she worries
about the youngest."
                          She cut
the deck, creating two half-decks
side by side on the table.
"I call you my oldest child,"
  she said and winked.
                          He gathered
the twin stacks and eased them
  into a single deck again.
She placed her hands on his
  so that he couldn't deal.
"You work too hard," she said,
  "and I don't want to live
  the rest of my life as a half-deck."
She kept her eyes on his
  until his eyes met hers,
  and still she gripped his hands.
At last his eyes confirmed
  what she was waiting for.
She freed his hands and smiled.
"Now what?" he asked.
                          "Deal."

Nothing Else to Add

"What did you say to Brian?"
"What could I say—," he answered,
   "I'm not good around grief."
They were driving back slowly
   from the funeral.
                  "I think
   our being there for him
   said everything," she added.
"I hope so."
               They had the look
   of a couple who had heard
   bad news once too often.
"How old was Janet?" she asked.
"Forty something—maybe fifty."
He steered into their driveway
   and parked but left the motor
   running.
               They sat in silence.
"It makes me wonder which one
   of us will die first," he mumbled.
"Don't talk like that."
                        He shut
   the motor off and faced her,
"What would you do if you
   were left alone?"
               He waited
   long enough to know that he'd asked
   the right question at the wrong
   time.
         "Some people say
   that women deal with loneliness
   better than men," he added.

"We're no different than men
   that way except we hide it
   better."
               "Would you ever
   marry again?"
                      "Are you
   being funny?"
                      "Just wondering . . ."
She took a deep breath and let
   it out audibly, "I think
   that people marry once—
   not only for the sex side of it
   but for everything that goes with it—
   feelings, decisions, promises,
   all of that."
                  "Does that mean
   no second marriage if the wife
   or husband dies?"
                  She drew
   another audible breath, "No matter
   which mate dies, the one that's left
   is like a two-wheeled car,
   unbalanced and going nowhere."
"Wouldn't another marriage
   reset the balance?"
                      "It might,
   but there'd always be a rearguard
   action with emotions, echoes . . . ,"
He knew her logic always trumped his
   on such subjects, but he went on,
"Does that apply if the first marriage
   was a bad marriage from the start?"
"In cases like that, it wasn't
   a marriage at all, was it?"
He opened the door a fraction and
   said, "There's one culture where

they have to kill the wife when
the husband dies and kill the
husband when the wife dies."
"Are you being funny again?"
"Just mentioning how some people
handle what we're talking about,"
he added as he shut the door
and sat like a stranger in his own skin
and almost whispered, "I was just
trying to lighten the mood."
"That's one subject that doesn't
lighten, Jim."
                    "What's the answer?"
She opened her door and stood
at her full height and said,
"I guess the only answer is
to live long enough to learn
what you never hoped to know."
He stared straight ahead
while she reached in and touched
his arm, "We're not there yet, dear,
so let's leave well enough alone
and have some fresh coffee
and finish cleaning out the attic."

Before Goodnight

"It's something we never discuss."
"It's not a subject that encourages
    discussion," he answered, "just acceptance."
She eased her nightgown over
    her head and let it downroll
    to her ankles.
                    "After Harriet
    lost her husband, " she said,
    "she turned old overnight."
"She probably felt young only
    with Fred, and when he died
    the spell was broken."
                    "Maybe
    we should prepare ourselves."
"No one can prepare for that."
She lay on the bed and stared
    at the ceiling.
                    "What would I do,"
    she asked, "if I woke up
    and you were gone forever?"
He was folding his pants on a hanger
    as if folding pants meant more
    than it meant.
                    Her eyes were closed
    when he faced around.
                    She lay
    so still he thought the worst
    had happened.
                    "Did you hear what
    I said," she asked and opened
    her eyes.

74

"I heard."

"It scares me
to think I'd be left to live on."
He hooked the hanger in the closet.
"Life and living on," she resumed,
    "are not the same."

"Maybe
your mood will change in the morning."
"Tolstoy was a liar."

"Tolstoy?"
"He said there's less charm in life
    when you think of death, but there's
    more peace."

"Isn't that true?"
"Not if you've lost your mate."
"You haven't lost me yet . . ."
"I hope I never do, sweetheart."
"Maybe Mrs. Tolstoy never said
    a thing like that to Tolstoy."
"If she didn't, she should have."

Re-Focus

"We rarely look in one another's
    eyes much anymore."
"It's not as if we never did,"
    he answered and grinned.

                        "But now
    I want each time we look
    to be like the first time."

                        "Or last,"
    he countered, and her smile faded.
She looked at him as if
    she thought his words a mockery
    and asked, "Why did you say that?"
"It just came out—I'm sorry."
He concentrated on the baked potato
    on his plate while she arranged
    and rearranged the napkin
    on her lap.

                "I didn't mean
    to spoil the moment, but I guess
    I did," he said and tried
    to touch her hand.

                        She spoke
    as if to some third party
    in the room, "I think that couples
    really stop seeing one another
    once they stop looking in each
    other's eyes."

                    "Is that an old
    saying you just made up?"
"It's true, regardless."

                        "Why?"

"Because the eyes can't lie,
    and lovers need that kind
    of reassurance all the time,
    or else they can't go on."
"Including us?"
                    "Of course."
"That's what I was trying to say
    when I said what I said."
"Say it again."
                    He pushed
    his plate aside so that
    nothing was between them
    as he said, "If every time
    should be the first, then any
    time could be the last,
    and that says everything."
"Is that your way of saying
    every time's the first
    and last—and only."
                    "Right."
"I never thought of it that way."
"What other way is there
    to think of it?"
                    After
    she turned and put her hand
    in his, they looked in one
    another's eyes so long it hurt.

Ballad of the Old Lovers

"Your body's slowed down, my dearest dear.
Your body's slowed down, my dearest."
"I'm aging, my dear—just aging, I fear.
Each day I keep growing older . . .
The birds in the trees may never freeze,
but the blood as you age grows colder."

"Remember the days when we used to play
and hug on the sheets of the bed there?
You'd touch me here and touch me here,
and then we would wrestle together?
Instead we lie now like the dead there
and listen all night to the weather."

"Remember the money we managed to save
and planned to enjoy in our sixties?
Well, sixty has come, and sixty has gone,
and what have our savings returned us
but travel in season without a good reason
and tropical sunlight that burned us?"

"Remember the friends we knew, we knew,
when we and our friends were younger?
Where have they gone, and why don't they write,
and why have the decades divided
all those not alive from those who survive
no matter how well they're provided?"

"But why blame our fears on the innocent years?
They're gone and beyond reliving.
Since death's quite efficient, and time's insufficient,

is it asking too much to forgive us
for wanting to stay till the end of the day
and love what the years can still give us?"

"So give me a kiss, my dearest of dears,
and sleep by my side forever.
Let the years come, and let the years go.
We treasure what nothing can sever.
In touch or apart is the same to the heart.
Until death parts us not, we're together."